W9-ABP-037

Living in Space

Today's World in Space

Living in Space

By David Baker

Rourke Enterprises, Inc.
Vero Beach, FL 32964

CONTENTS

First Steps

The first manned space flights that carried *astronauts* into orbit were able to support life for only a few hours. The astronauts flew in spacecraft that were small, cramped, and primitive. Nobody knew how to build a spacecraft. No one knew if people could survive a rocket launch and the weightlessness of space. All these questions had to be answered before astronauts could live and work in space.

NASA, The National Aeronautics and Space Administration, was formed in 1958 to look after America's civilian space program. The military already had space programs, but these were for national security instead of science. President Eisenhower wanted America to explore space for the benefit of all people, and NASA was set up to do that.

Before NASA could know what sort of goal to seek, it had to find out what happened to people in space. The only way to do that was to send people up and measure their reactions. The first

Called Mercury, the first U.S. manned spacecraft was a tiny vehicle only six feet in diameter.

Gordon Cooper checks out his instruments and displays aboard the Mercury spacecraft before his flight in 1963.

manned vehicles, therefore, were designed just to prove that getting into space and returning to Earth again was technically possible. The program was risky, however, because no one knew for sure what the pilot would find.

In 1959, NASA began searching for astronauts. The word astronaut comes from astronautics, the science of space travel and space vehicles. Where would NASA look for such people? The logical choice was to look at pilots trained by the U.S. Air Force and the U.S. Navy. Both had several test pilot schools where men were trained to test new planes and develop better designs for future applications.

Mercury was launched by the Atlas missile converted into a satellite launcher; it was to put four Mercury capsules in orbit during 1962 and 1963.

The Atlas launch vehicle put great stress on pilots who flew Mercury capsules into space because of the high rate of acceleration and vibration.

To give physicians a better understanding of the effects of weightlessness on living things, monkeys and apes were frequently sent into space to test conditions before men orbited the Earth.

These men were used to the unknown and had an intelligent respect for danger. They were not easily shaken and could react quickly to unusual situations. Moreover, they were physically fit, used to long hours in classrooms learning about new technology, and had an appetite for new challenges. NASA put out a request and received several thousand applications from the armed services and civilian test pilots.

NASA finally narrowed down the applicants to just a few. The space agency recruited seven men, and the training began. These seven men were the first U.S. astronauts, and they were picked to fly the tiny Mercury spacecraft. It was just about big enough to take one man with little room to spare. The first time an American astronaut rode a rocket into space was on May 5 1961, when Alan Shepard sat in his Mercury capsule on top of a Redstone missile. He was rocketed into space for a 15-minute trip to a height of more than 100 miles. A repeat test followed several months later with Virgil Grissom in the capsule.

The Mercury space suit had a diagonal zipper across the chest and a circular neck ring which supported the protective helmet.

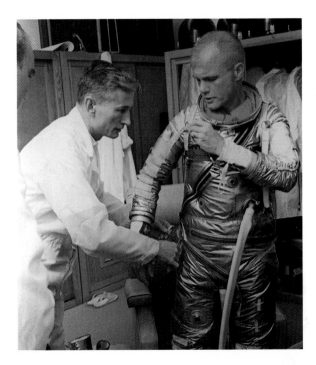

The flights into *orbit* began with John Glenn in February 1962 and were followed by three more involving Malcolm Scott Carpenter, Walter Schirra, and Gordon Cooper. The Mercury project came to an end in 1963. Six astronauts had been into space. One, Donald Slayton, was thought to have a heart problem, but he would walk on the moon in 1971. Mercury proved that man could live in the weightless environment of space. This small step led to more dramatic goals ahead.

In May 1961, less than three weeks after Alan Shepard returned from his first Redstone ride, President Kennedy challenged Americans to reach the moon by the end of the decade. No one

Although much bigger than Mercury, because Gemini carried two astronauts there was still not much room for each person to move around.

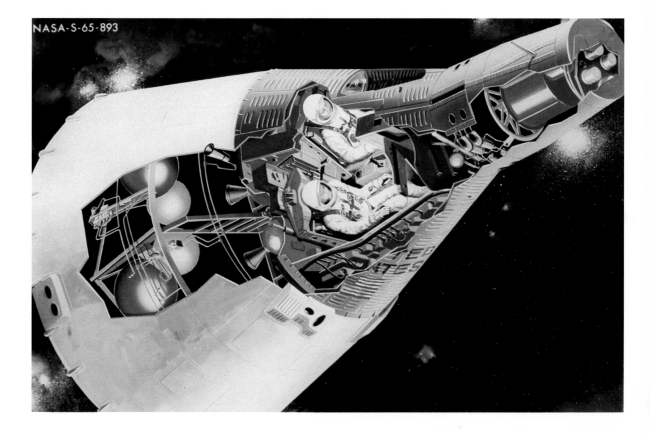

NASA-S-65-893

Beginning in 1965, NASA flew ten two-man missions with the Gemini spacecraft.

knew at the time how that goal could be accomplished, and a second manned spacecraft, Gemini, was built to test different techniques that would be necessary for a mission to the moon. Astronauts would have to walk in space protected only by their space suits, they would have to meet up with and dock to other vehicles in space, and they would have to survive for about two weeks between launch and landing.

The Gemini program needed more astronauts, and NASA was soon at work recruiting pilots. Astronauts who gained experience in Gemini would go on to fly in the moon landing program called Apollo. The Gemini spacecraft was bigger than Mercury, but it carried two astronauts who would remain in space for up to fourteen days. In ten manned missions during 1965 and 1966, the foundation

for future space travel was laid down. Astronauts walked in space and demonstrated they could perform useful work, spacecraft were docked together, and physicians learned a lot about the human body.

Comfort conditions aboard Gemini, said one astronaut, were like two people crawling into sleeping bags and living in a telephone booth for two weeks. It was small, and the crew members were unable to get out of their seats although they could move around them in them a bit. Everything they did had to be done in the semi-sitting position. They had space suits on to protect them from a puncture in the wall of the spacecraft. Like the cabin of an aircraft, the crew compartment was pressurized, but wearing the suits was an added safety measure. Besides, the suits were essential for going outside, and there was no room to take them off.

Weightlessness

The human body is designed for life at the surface of the Earth and is not built for weightlessness. Earth has a field of *gravity* that pulls everything down toward the center of the planet. Our bodies are adapted to this phenomenon, and difficulties arise if they are removed from this field of gravity. The flow of blood around the body, the use of muscle to resist gravity, and the growth of bone marrow are all affected by gravity or lack of gravity.

Scientists knew that problems would be created in the human body when people started going into space. They did not know to what extent weightlessness would affect the body, and

they limited the duration of early space flights. The flights gradually got longer, and doctors monitored the crew carefully before approving the next stage in long-duration flight.

The longest Mercury flight lasted just over a day, but the Soviets had already flown a mission that lasted almost five days. The second Gemini flight extended the time in space to four days; it was the start of a sequence of two-man flights designed to unravel any medical problems that might appear. Because medical research was one of the main objectives of the program, the spacecraft had been designed for two men. If an astronaut got into difficulty, his life might depend upon the help of his colleague.

The next flight lasted eight days, and another mission went for fourteen days. Fourteen days was necessary to fly to the moon, stay for a day or

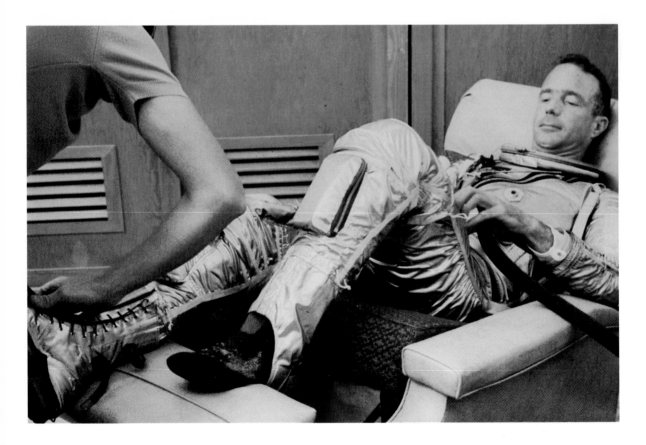

Space suits worn by astronauts in the Mercury program were a protection in case the capsule was punctured by a micrometeorite.

several side effects. The bones would become brittle, the heart would slowly lose its ability to do useful work, and the changes in blood cells would affect the ability of the bones to produce calcium.

After Apollo, astronauts increased their stay in space by flying to the Skylab space station placed in orbit in 1973. During 1973 and 1974, three teams of astronauts visited Skylab. The last team remained in space for 84 days, the

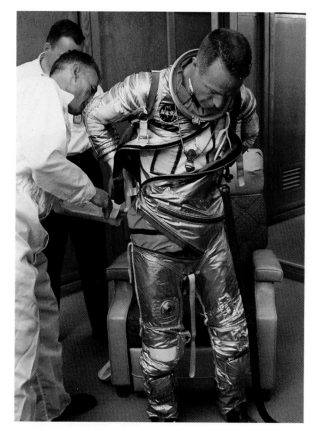

The main part of the space suit was made in one piece with pressure-sealed zippers to make the suit air-tight.

Virgil I. (Gus) Grissom in his pressure-sealed space suit ready to go to the pad for launch.

so, and return to Earth. The moon program had top priority, and there was no time to continue with even longer missions. Gemini proved it was physically possible for humans to remain in space for the duration of a moon flight, and further research into the medical effects of long-duration missions would wait until the moon landing program was over.

What did scientists learn from Gemini? For starters, they discovered four things about the reaction of the body to weightlessness. Bone loses minerals at a steady rate related to the time spent in space, blood cells change, the body loses large amounts of fluid, and muscles become weak. These four primary effects had

Physicians learned more about the body's reaction to weightlessness when men went outside their spacecraft on space walks.

longest U.S. manned space flight. Skylab was huge and provided ample space for medical experiments. In Gemini and Apollo, medical research was carried out by watching the changes to the body after a space flight. Very little could be done to monitor the astronauts in space.

All that changed with Skylab. Several large pieces of medical equipment were installed on Skylab, including a device to measure the movement of blood around the body. On Earth, gravity causes blood to pool in the lower part of the body. In a weightless condition, the blood floats upward, and more blood pools in the upper part of the body, including the head. The

Gordon Cooper gets a welcome breath of fresh air as his spacecraft is picked up after a manned orbital flight in 1963.

blood presses on the walls of the heart, and the heart, reacting as if the person has high blood pressure, cuts down the production of body fluids. This is why astronauts lose weight upon going into space.

Veteran astronauts of both Mercury and Gemini space flights, Walter M. Schirra (left) pauses for a thoughtful conversation with Virgil I. (Gus) Grissom.

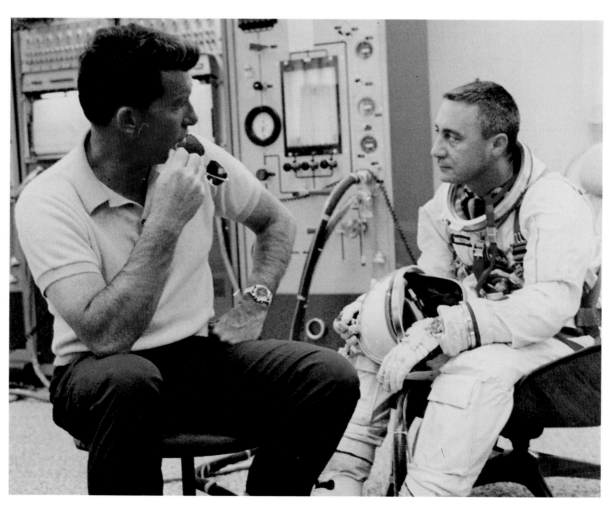

During a space walk, an astronaut was wired up with special instruments that sent information to Earth about heart beat and breathing rate.

Another Skylab medical instrument was designed to help the astronauts retain muscle by doing hard work. The crew members operated a bicycle exerciser fixed to the floor of the space station. Special instruments monitored their heart rate and recorded daily changes in the ability of the heart to do useful work. Several hours' exercise a day was necessary to maintain the same physical condition as on Earth.

One Skylab experiment was designed to observe the effects of weightlessness on balance and orientation. The body sensor that tells a person whether he or she is up or down is located in the region of the ear. Fluid reacts with gravity to send messages to the brain and balance the person on two legs, or even one.

Without gravity, does the person become totally disoriented and lose balance? Skylab was the size of a small house, and there was plenty of room to carry out tests to learn the answer.

The Skylab experiment consisted of a rotating chair. The astronaut was slowly spun around while his eyes were covered. While the astronaut attempted to carry out simple tasks, such as reaching out to touch things, the physicians measured the distance his arm had moved to reach objects placed in front of him. They then could observe his ability to maintain balance and coordination. Results showed that disorientation was not a serious problem, and with training it could be overcome.

Skylab was abandoned when the last crew returned home in 1974. It had given NASA

Although Gemini was a great improvement over Mercury, there was little room inside the spacecraft to move around and do exercises that help counter the effects of weightlessness.

The three-man Apollo spacecraft, used to carry astronauts from Earth to moon orbit and back, had much more room than earlier vehicles.

The largest spacecraft of all was the Skylab space station, launched in 1973 and manned by three teams of visiting astronauts.

astronauts up to three months of continuous occupation. The medical results answered many questions about the effects of very long flights on the human body. Moon flights lasted just a few days. Flights to Mars would last nine months each way. Space travel to the planets could take place only if the human body was able to withstand long periods without gravity.

The results of Skylab seemed to indicate that there would be a limit. Was that limit less than the nine months needed to fly to Mars? The answer would come when Soviet cosmonauts spent a year in space during 1988 and returned safely to Earth. The United States, meanwhile, pressed ahead with other manned projects like the shuttle, which cannot remain in space longer than two weeks. The long-duration effects of weightlessness will be studied again when NASA assembles a permanently manned space station in orbit during the late 1990s. Until then, most of the work will be left to the Soviets.

Sleep

The first astronauts that went into space did not remain long enough to go to sleep. The first three Mercury orbital missions lasted a maximum of nine hours. The sixth and last Mercury mission in 1963 was extended to 34 hours, and on this flight astronaut Gordon Cooper went to sleep. He slept in several periods, dozing when there was little other work to do. A couple of times he awoke without knowing where he was for several seconds.

Seen here after splashdown, the inside of a Gemini spacecraft provided little room to curl up and go to sleep; astronauts had to sleep where they lay on their couches.

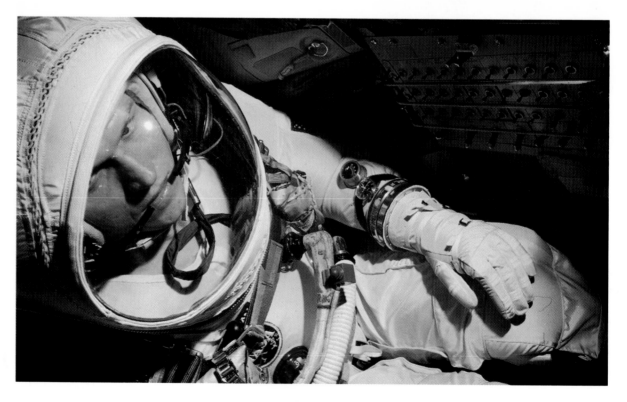

Survival during the two weeks spent in orbit by *Gemini 7* astronauts Borman and Lovell was made possible through the use of a special soft space suit, which could be removed for greater comfort.

Learning how to work in the weightlessness of space, astronauts rehearse underwater with a full size mock-up of tasks they will carry out in space.

The flights in the Gemini program were of much longer duration, and all except two remained at least several days in space. Special studies on sleep patterns were carried out. Astronauts wore special sensors on their heads to record the length of time they were asleep and the depth of the sleep. Scientists measure sleep in various stages, and they found astronauts sleep deeply for about the first two hours and then gradually less deep until they wake.

The commanders slept more restlessly than their colleagues because they felt responsible for the spacecraft and their fellow crew members. They were less able to go into deep sleep and woke frequently to check the spacecraft systems and make sure their buddies were all right. The spacecraft was their life-giving protection against the hostile environment of space. Only a thin steel shell separated them from disaster, and this thought never seemed to be far from their minds during sleep time.

In Mercury and Gemini there was no room at all to move about the cabin and take off space suits. The astronauts simply slept where they were. Apollo provided a little more room for the three astronauts, and NASA provided sleeping bags for the first time in a spacecraft. Apollo had three couches suspended by struts to absorb the shock of landing. Sleeping bags were designed to be hung like hammocks under the couches. In

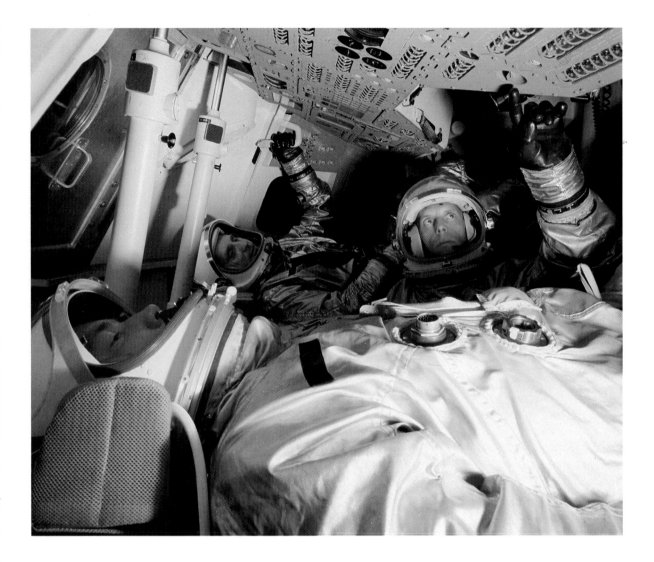

fact, the astronauts usually found a corner of the spacecraft and just curled up and slept right there.

By the time Skylab came along more than a decade after Mercury, the astronauts enjoyed real luxury. Skylab contained sleep cubicles, where each astronaut had the privacy of a curtained-off closet. Hanging from the wall like bats, each crew member had a sleeping bag that kept arms and legs from drifting around. More than once an astronaut woke up with a start to find his arms floating around in front of his face. Skylab astronauts also had books to read and music to listen to in their personal sleep closets.

Apollo astronauts could remove their suits and stow them; they could rest in hammocks under the couches.

For the first time, astronauts could live more like human beings than guinea pigs. They had regular work days, rest days, and times to relax. Scientists watched these cycles of work and play very closely. It would help decide how much work

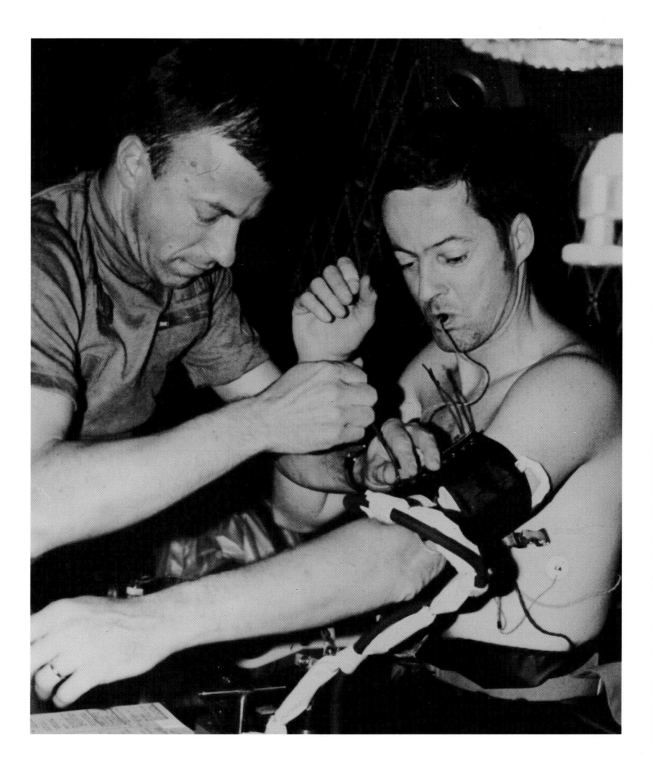

Monitoring the effects of weightlessness and sleeping conditions on long space missions was an important part of understanding how the body reacts to this new environment.

Future astronauts will work and rest aboard permanently manned stations housing several other astronauts, sometimes from different countries. The ability to get along with other crew members was an important part of the early manned space programs. It was even more important aboard Skylab, where astronauts spent several weeks with each other. The correct balance between sleep, rest, work, and play is an important part of keeping harmony aboard the station.

In the much roomier Skylab, an astronaut hangs weightless like a bat inside a cupboard.

people can do in space and how much rest they need. Astronauts on Skylab tended to be highly motivated. They slept less than they would on Earth without apparent ill effects, and they frequently gave up their rest day to press ahead with scientific experiments.

Getting astronauts to rest can be a real problem. Space is a place where many exciting things can happen. Every day brings a new experience, and the fascination of living and working in a weightless environment is stimulating. People need rest and relaxation if they are to improve their efficiency at work. This is no less important aboard a space station than it is on Earth. The mind needs challenges and tasks to do, but it also needs variety and stimulation.

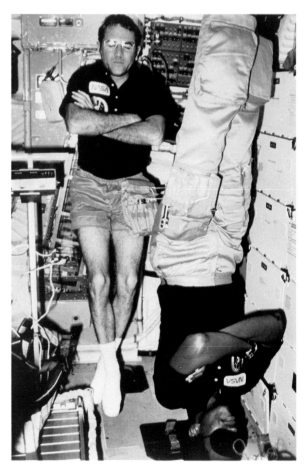

Astronauts in the shuttle have all the room they need to stretch out and sleep comfortably wherever they like.

24

Mealtime

Eating food in space has always been an essential part of space flight. The human body cannot function properly without a balanced diet — regular food of good quality with the right nutritional content. Space scientists and engineers knew this, and they worked with physicians and nutritional specialists to cater to the needs of the astronaut. The challenge was not so much to provide the right amount of vitamins and nutrients, but to provide an appealing meal with variety and change.

For many people, eating is more than a necessity. It is a pleasure to be enjoyed. Away from the comforts of planet Earth in a steel case orbiting outside the atmosphere, mealtime can be a stimulus to relaxation and satisfaction. It is as important as adequate rest and sleep time. The pleasurable aspects of space food were not available to the first astronauts, however. Their food was provided in a basic and practical manner.

Shuttle astronauts have the advantage of lockers and drawers carrying cans and containers with a wide variety of food and drink.

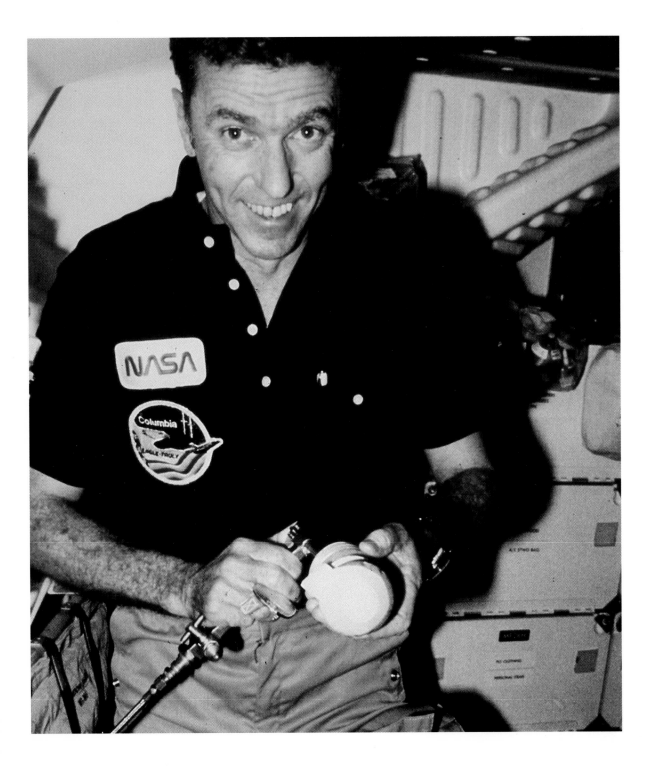

Some food is taken into space with all the water removed and water is added when the
meal is about to be taken.

Weight was always a problem for engineers. Extra weight in the spacecraft meant extra rocket power had to be provided to get the vehicle in space. Later, when weight and volume restrictions were relaxed, astronauts could enjoy a wider variety of food and a more convenient way of eating it.

In the early days, food consisted of strained meats, vegetables, and fruit packed in collapsible containers. Astronauts sucked the contents through a tube in the faceplate of their suit helmets. They also had bite-sized cubes of food coated in edible fat to prevent crumbs. Spacecraft have many switches to operate, and sticky crumbs were not good items to have floating around during a long flight.

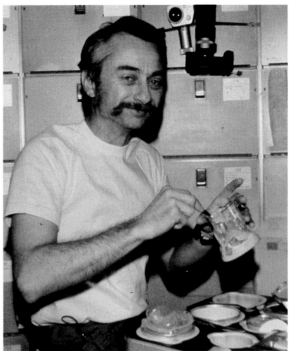

Astronaut Owen K. Garriott begins a meal aboard Skylab during his 59 days in space.

The first astronaut to eat in space was John Glenn. On the first orbital flight in 1962, he ate apple sauce squeezed from an aluminum tube. After that, things got progressively better. In Gemini, astronauts had a selection of three types of food: bite-sized cubes of meat, fruit, dessert, and bread; semi-moist foods; and dehydrated foods that were made digestible by adding water.

Dehydrated foods were contained in packets. Water was injected through a small hole at one corner, and the astronaut massaged the contents until they became palatable. They frequently were not. Large lumps often remained and got stuck in the water hole, which was also the place where the astronaut tried to suck out the contents. Two different daily menus were carried, and the astronauts alternated between them.

An astronaut sucks on a Pepsi bottle, taking a refreshing drink between tasks.

Astronauts Young and Merbold take a meal in the mid-deck area of the shuttle during the STS-9 mission in 1983.

A typical Gemini meal day would begin with bacon squares, chicken sandwiches, gingerbread, peanut cubes, and grapefruit juice. This meal provided a total of 848 calories. The second meal consisted of beef bites, apricot cubes, date cake, cinnamon toast, and orange or grapefruit juice, a total of 809 calories. The last meal of the day included beef sandwiches, pineapple fruit cake, peanut cubes, and grapefruit juice. This had 792 calories.

Total calorie intake for a typical day aboard Gemini was 2,449. This is slightly less than an average man requires on Earth, because

nutritionists felt that the astronauts world be doing less work in space. Slightly fewer calories would achieve a balance between food going in and energy being expended. Apollo astronauts had a wider selection of food and special spoon-bowl food. This allowed astronauts to eat some items with a spoon, after it had been moistened with water.

Skylab provided food packed in individual portions in aluminum cans with a protective plastic cover that kept the food in the can when it was opened. Meals were served on trays that had special receptacles to plug into heaters. The

Shuttle operations usually require one astronaut to prepare the day's meals for all crew members and this duty is taken in turn.

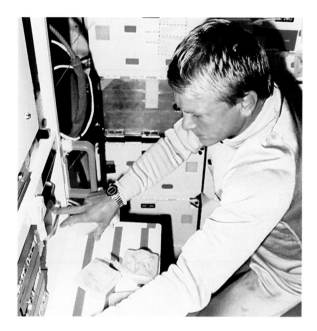

Skylab food system was a great improvement over that on earlier spacecraft. Skylab carried just over a ton of food for three astronauts to last a period of 140 days. There would be three visits to the station by separate teams of astronauts.

Skylab astronauts ate about 3,000 calories per day. Food was kept in eleven special lockers,

For the first four shuttle missions, astronauts were given only a primitive package of food, juices, and drinks.

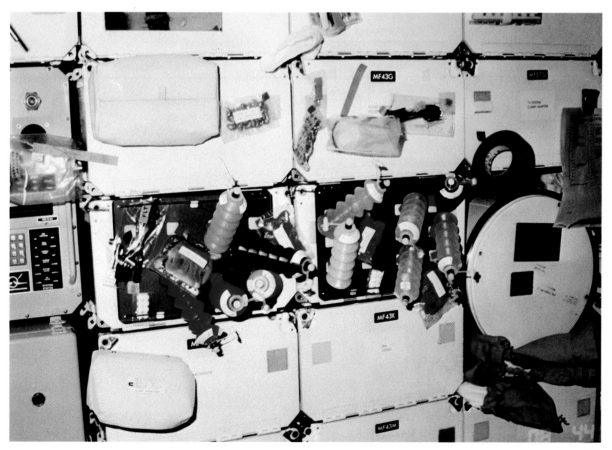

and frozen items were kept in five freezers. A crew member was assigned chef for the day and would prepare the meals for his colleagues. Very strict control was kept on the dietary balance of vitamins and nutrients. If they did not eat all the food at a particular meal, the astronauts took a tablet. This would supplement any deficiency and maintain the planned level of vitamins.

The food aboard the shuttle is even better than that on Skylab, but there are no freezers on board. The shuttle is intended for relatively short-duration flights of about a week, and there is no need for large stocks. Up to eight astronauts have flown on a single mission, however. That is equivalent to having only three astronauts on Skylab for almost three weeks. The

SHUTTLE OPS

MEAL TRAY

The fifth shuttle mission saw the first use of a new meal-packaging system for food, much like the containers used for airline passengers.

On the ninth shuttle mission, NASA began to use this modified tray, which is easier to handle in weightlessness.

shuttle does have a galley with a hot air oven. Unfortunately, this oven has been a constant problem on the shuttle and has rarely worked properly.

A typical shuttle day might begin with a meal of peaches, beef pattie, scrambled eggs, bran flakes, cocoa, and orange drink. The next meal would include corned beef, asparagus, bread, pears, peanuts, and lemonade. The final meal of the day would consist of beef with barbeque sauce, cauliflower cheese, beans with mushrooms, lemon pudding, pecan cookies, and cocoa. The day's intake of calories would be around 3,000, about the same as Skylab.

Bathroom Chores

Health and cleanliness is as important in space as on Earth. On Earth, it can prevent disease, help us enjoy life more, and build a better body for greater fitness. It can help us develop a more active brain for improved efficiency. In space, astronaut efficiency and performance is vital. Adequate sleep and proper food is just one part of a chain of healthy living that must be maintained in space as it is on the ground. Other important areas are the all-important bathroom duties.

The simple act of washing is easy on Earth, but in space it is accompanied by a host of problems that must be overcome. Without

This full size mock-up of the interior of Skylab shows the galley (left corner), the bathroom (lower center) and the three sleeping cubicles (right center) with the open exercise area at the top.

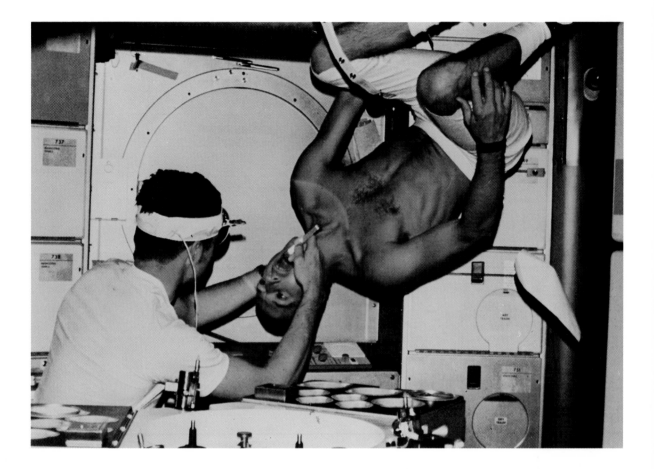

Astronauts won't get tooth decay through eating candy, but they may need dental treatment on very long missions.

gravity, water simply gathers in globules and floats around. There is no means of easily gathering it up, and it can be dangerous if some of it escapes, especially with electrical equipment around. Astronauts on early missions had very little space to use for washing, and the tiny living area made normal bathroom duties extremely difficult.

Cleanliness was difficult under such cramped conditions, but towels and wet wipes were provided. Every effort was made to keep the spacecraft as clean as possible, but this was especially difficult on the longer flights. There was little improvement with Apollo, since that spacecraft was as cramped as Gemini. Only with Skylab was the space available for a proper bathroom. A water jet was provided to dampen a towel for washing, but it took some practice to get used to.

Shaving in space was once thought to be a very dangerous activity. Millions of tiny bristles floating around are about as welcome in a spacecraft as globules of water. Some even thought it would be a health hazard, and that

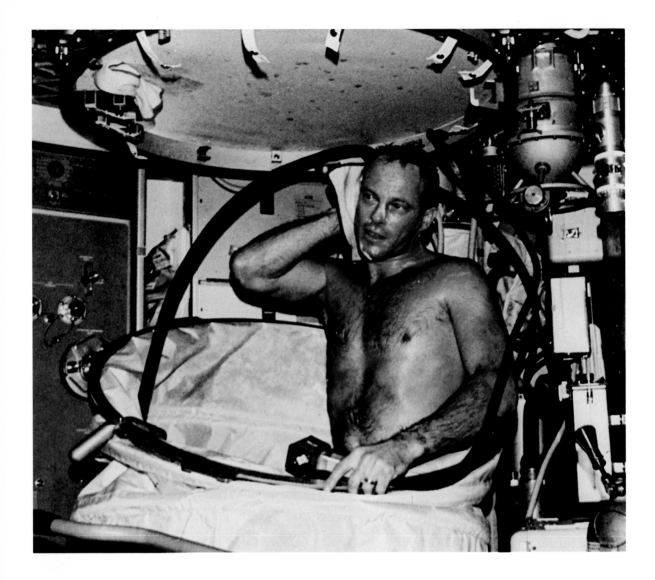

Skylab astronaut Jack R. Lousma takes a shower from a water spray inside a sealed bag attached to the ceiling of the space station.

astronauts could inhale these hairs through the nose. An electric razor that captured all the shaved bristle was tried, but that did not work well at all. Finally, a cream was tried for a proper wet shave, and that has been used ever since.

Taking a bath in space is even harder than shaving. Not before Skylab did a spacecraft have the room for such luxury. Skylab, however, did have a shower, and it worked quite well. The water was sprayed inside a completely enclosed drum made of fabric. The astronaut simply floated inside and pulled it up over his head. The water jet was then connected and turned on. A special suction device at the other end drew the water drops out, and the astronaut then toweled himself off.

34

Even in space, an astronaut needs to shave every day.

The shuttle is not equipped to carry a shower, and the flights are not long enough to make it necessary. A shower will be installed, however, in the space station NASA will build in the late 1990s. A shower will be essential, since astronauts are expected to remain in space for period of three months at a time. The space station shower will be an improved version of the Skylab shower. At the end of the day, this may be the one piece of equipment the space station crew refuses to live without.

There is plenty of room aboard the modern spacecraft for personal hygiene packs.

Soviets in Space

The Soviet Union operates the world's largest space program. It routinely launches about 120 satellites and spacecraft each year. The rest of the world, including the United States, launches a total of 30 to 40. For many years the Soviets have been carrying out research into long-duration space flight. For a while, NASA had the lead in this kind of research. That lead ended when the last Skylab astronauts came back from their twelve weeks in space during February 1974.

In 1978, two Soviet cosmonauts came home after exceeding this record with a flight of more than thirteen weeks. They had remained aboard the Salyut space station. Salyut was a series of space stations, each about 49 feet long with a maximum diameter of 13 feet, 6 inches. They were much smaller than Skylab and could

The Soviets have operated a series of space stations since 1971, in which they have experimented with long-duration flight.

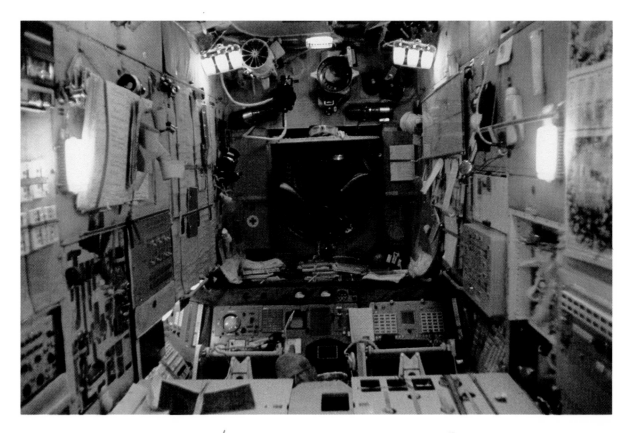

Their latest space station is called *Mir;* during 1988 two cosmonauts spent a year in orbit in this area.

comfortably house no more than two cosmonauts. The first Salyut was launched as early as 1971, but success was slow to come and long-duration flights did not begin for several years.

Following the 13-week flight in 1978, the Soviets gradually built up long-duration time in space. Later the same year they ran a flight for almost 20 weeks, and in 1979 they operated a crew aboard Salyut for 25 weeks. That was followed by another flight lasting 30 weeks in 1982. Flight durations increased over the next several years until, in 1988, a single two-man crew remained in space for a complete year. By this time the Salyut had been modified and renamed *Mir,* which means "peace" in Russian.

The Soviets' experience in long-duration

flight led to many rumors that they were rehearsing for a flight to Mars. They are certainly interested in exploring that planet and have sent some very advanced robots to explore the surface. What the Soviet research has shown is that people can remain in a weightless condition for many months, longer than the time required to reach Mars. Actually getting there will be a very different matter.

Living in space means more than being able to resist the medical effects of weightlessness. It means being able to remain alive independent of Earth. The Soviets have done many experiments in plant growth for orbital stations. Eventually this research may lead to the production of food aboard stations. Only then will plans for a trip to Mars be practical.

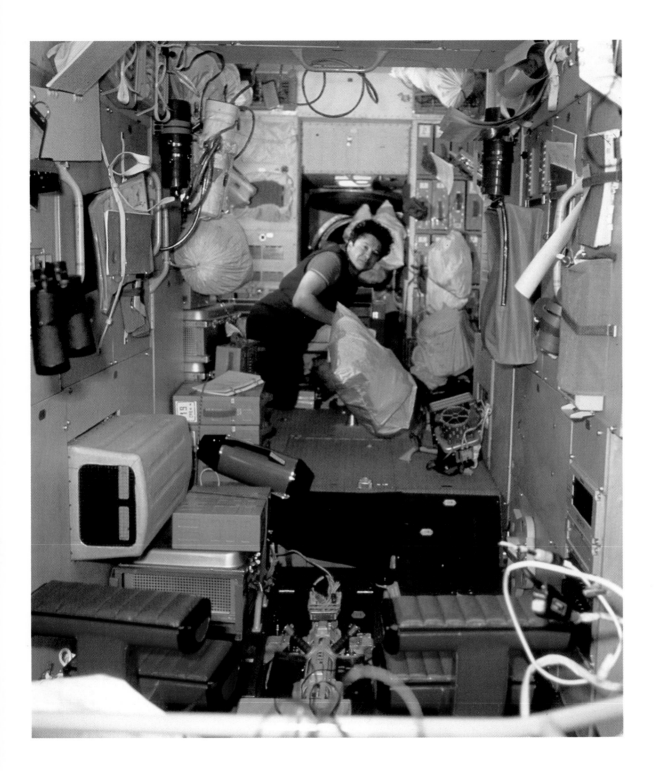

Mir may look big, but if the wing-like solar panels were removed from the outside, the entire station could be put inside the cargo bay of the shuttle.

Space Station

NASA is designing a space station that will be assembled in Earth orbit at the end of the 1990s. It will provide the first permanent U.S. facility in orbit for continuous scientific research. Research will no longer take place on a mission-by-mission basis, but all the time. The new space station will always have working astronauts aboard, and it will be a stepping stone to space colonies of the future. Astronauts and scientists that work there will come from several countries.

Europe, Canada, and Japan have joined with the United States to operate this station. It will have four *pressurized modules*. One, built by the U.S., will be where crew members live, sleep, eat, and rest. The second module will be the U.S. *experiment module*. Additional experiment modules, about the same size, will be built by Europe and Japan. Canada is building a *satellite repair station* to be attached to the outside framework.

By the mid-1990s NASA expects to have a space station in orbit 300 miles above Earth where astronauts can live on a permanent basis.

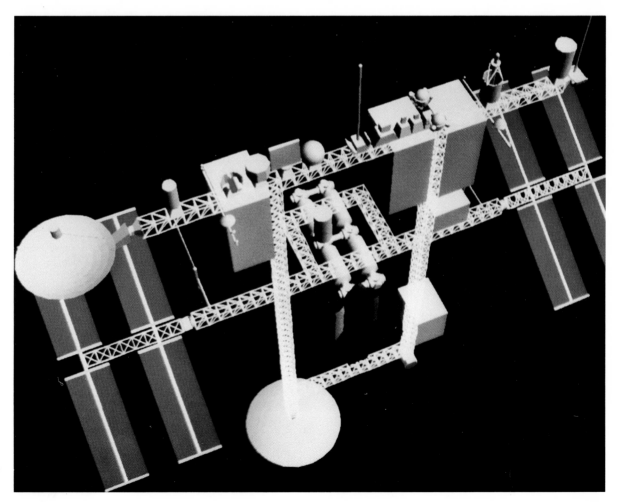

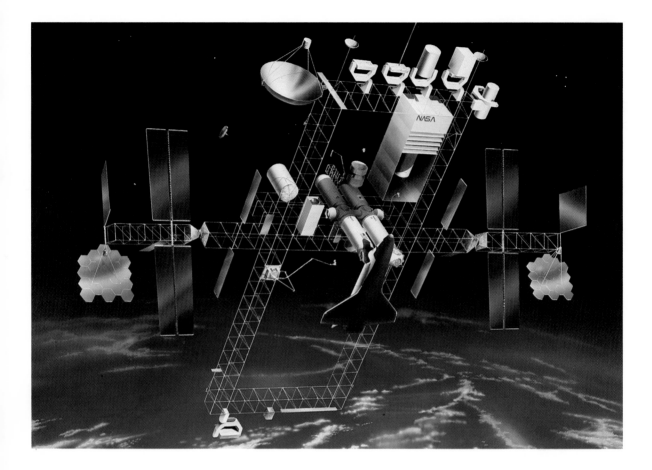

The space station will provide comfortable living quarters for up to six people at a time, although eight or ten could be aboard the station for brief periods when crews change over. A normal tour of duty would probably last three months, although long-duration medical tests will be carried out on some astronauts who could remain aboard the station indefinitely. Some of the crew members will be responsible for control and operation of the station, while others will be there as scientists to carry out specific experiments.

Living and working in space in the first decade of the next century will be very different from life aboard the shuttle. Although comfortable compared with earlier spacecraft, the shuttle is a

Over time, the station will expand to provide more services for scientists and engineers working in space high above the Earth.

short-duration transport vehicle for moving people and cargo between the surface of the Earth and a more permanent station in space. The station will be made comfortable, and it will contain good color balance to make astronauts feel at home.

Crew members will want to talk with their families on Earth. On previous missions, test pilots knew they were flying a specific mission for a brief period. Only nine U.S. astronauts have remained in space longer than two weeks. Scientists and engineers will make flights to the station for thirteen weeks at a time. They will not want to be out of contact with their families for that period, and provisions will be made to ease their loneliness.

Life aboard an orbiting station will be busy but calm. It will require tolerance and compromise. Many different nationalities will live and work together. Privacy will be important, and astronauts will sometimes want to read quietly or listen to music. The space station will be a testing ground for another challenge: the first flight to the planets. That can only take place when scientists learn more about how people live in space and get along together for long periods.

The space station modules will look something like this, with living quarters in the long module on top and scientific experiments being carried out in the long module at the bottom.

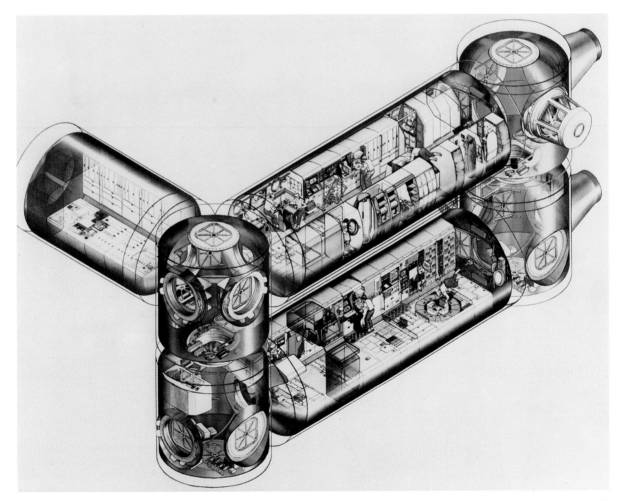

Increasingly, robots working outside the vehicle will relieve astronauts of tedious jobs.

The station will grow and expand as its needs change with time. It is designed to remain in space for at least twenty years. Continual modification to the station and occasional repairs will be necessary facts of life. Astronauts will have to go outside occasionally to tend experiments on special *platforms*. It will be the first true colony out of this world.

The design for a space station shower is tested out under simulated weightless conditions, achieved for about 30 seconds by an aircraft diving steeply toward the ground.

In the Future

Some day space stations may be placed in several different locations. Some may be put into *polar orbits* that cover the entire surface of the planet as the Earth spins on its axis. Passing over both the north and the south poles in turn, a station in this path would watch the planet slowly revolve beneath it. This would give a total view of the Earth over several days and enable astronauts to monitor the health of crops, the rise and fall of flood waters, or the spread of pollution.

Other stations high above the Earth may service satellites going back and forth between low and high orbits. *Science satellites* may have their lives extended when small space shuttles drag them to the station for refueling or repair. An entire colony will be supported by a network of small *space taxis*, traveling back and forth like barges on the Mississippi River.

In time, station modules may become the shelters for the first colonies on the moon and Mars. Lessons about living and working in space would be applied, and it would be a little easier to carry out work. The moon has one-sixth the gravity of Earth while Mars has one-third the gravity of our home planet. The elaborate technology which would have to evolve to support these frontier outposts would make life pleasant.

Scientists set up a temporary inflatable living dome on Eros, an asteroid between the planets Mars and Jupiter.

Astro-scientists detonate a small explosive charge to measure the effect of shock waves on the rocks as they explore Saturn's largest moon, Titan.

The ordinary processes of eating, sleeping, washing, and playing that we take for granted on the surface of the Earth are being relearned by space travelers. They are, in a way, new beings in a new world, and they have to go through all the stages of learning basic functions once again.

We have no idea where our explorations will lead, nor where they will end. We are preparing for the exploration of the solar system and manned colonies on the moon and Mars. We have already taken a giant step since the days when a man stepped into a capsule and blasted into space for the first time. From that act came our first toehold on the moon. Soon, we will have our first residents aboard the space station in orbit. We are Earthlings with a cosmic future.

Ultimately, astronauts will work on other planets, like these astronauts performing experiments on Mars' frozen ice caps.

GLOSSARY

Astronaut	People who are trained to fly in space. The word comes from astronautics, the science of space travel and space vehicles.
Experiment module	A space station module built for scientific equipment and day-to-day research in orbit.
Gravity	The force of attraction that moves or tends to move bodies toward the center of a celestial body such as the Earth or moon.
NASA	National Aeronautics and Space Administration, set up in October 1958 for the peaceful exploration of space.
Orbit	The curved path, usually almost circular, followed by a planet or satellite in its motion around another planet in space.
Platforms	Space platforms are used for experiments that have special requirements and cannot be kept in the main space station.
Polar orbit	An orbital path that takes a spacecraft over a planet or star's poles.
Pressurized modules	Space station modules pressurized with a mixture of oxygen and nitrogen, controlled in a temperature to simulate the Earth-like environment.
Satellite repair station	A place on the space station where satellites can be berthed for repair by robots or space-walking astronauts.
Science satellites	Satellites placed in low Earth orbit designed to observe the universe, the atmosphere, or the surface of the Earth.
Space taxis	Small rocket-powered vehicles kept in Earth orbit for ferrying modules and cargo between orbits.

INDEX

Page numbers in *italics* refer to photographs or illustrations.